Three-dimensional
Découpage

~

INNOVATIVE PROJECTS FOR BEGINNERS

Three-dimensional Découpage

INNOVATIVE PROJECTS FOR BEGINNERS

Hilda Stokes

GUILD OF MASTER CRAFTSMAN PUBLICATIONS LTD

First published 2003 by
Guild of Master Craftsman Publications Ltd,
166 High Street, Lewes,
East Sussex, BN7 1XU

Text © Hilda Stokes 2003
© in the work GMC Publications Ltd

ISBN 1 86108 370 X

A catalogue record of this book is available from the British Library.

Publisher: Paul Richardson
Art Director: Ian Smith
Production Manager: Matt Weyland
Managing Editor: April McCroskie
Editor: Dominique Page
Designer: Fran Rawlinson
Photographer: Anthony Bailey

Typeface: Tiepolo and Adobe Garamond

Colour origination by Universal Graphics, Pte Ltd, Singapore

Printed and bound by Kyodo Printing, Pte Ltd, Singapore

Dedication

This book is dedicated to my husband, Freddy. Without his support this book would never have been possible.

ACKNOWLEDGEMENTS

I would like to thank my two daughters, Emma and Katharine, for their endless encouragement.

My good friend and neighbour, Mr Cliff Ingham, made a beautiful table for the 'Morning-glory' project, and I would like to thank him for all the long hours he spent in his workshop. Thank you Cliff!

My grateful thanks also go to John Arnold Publishing, and Bryan and Chrissie Hall for allowing me to use their prints, and to Simon Elvin Limited for giving their kind permission to use their giftwrap.

Contents

~

~

The Projects

Introduction

'Découpage' is derived from the French *découper*, which means 'to cut out', and that is exactly what this book is all about: cutting up paper, prints and giftwrap in order to create some of the most beautiful and original pictures.

I first encountered three-dimensional découpage in a little craft shop. I thought the work was lovely and decided to take up the craft myself. I enrolled on a one-day course and spent several enjoyable hours learning how to cut, mould and glue. By the end of the day I had completed a picture of a fuchsia, and was so proud that I presented it to everyone on my return home.

After the course, I practised each day; and over the years I have gradually developed my own way with the craft. Now, friends and acquaintances often ask me to create pictures for special occasions, such as birthdays, christenings or weddings. I must confess, I am completely addicted – I will try to découpage anything printed on paper, even napkins!

To help you, I have prepared cutting guides, plus a list of basic supplies that you will require. I have also provided a list of suppliers at the back of the book, detailing where you can obtain the prints and giftwrap I have used, though of course you can apply the principles of découpage explained in this book to any design you choose.

It is quite unlikely that you will need to buy any special tools, as most of the equipment can usually be found in the home. However, the materials can be expensive. The finished result, though, is so rewarding that it's worth the expense, especially when your friends enquire whether your picture is porcelain or enamelled.

This craft is also known as Paper Tole or Paper Sculpting, but whatever name you prefer, it's a beautiful pastime that is both absorbing and restful. To enjoy it, all you need is a little time on your hands and some patience. And remember, do not despair if your first attempts fail – you will improve the more you practise!

Tools and Materials

The following list comprises the tools and materials you will need in order to complete the projects in this book.

1. Approximately five prints of the same design
2. Felt-tipped pens and watercolours
3. Manicure scissors with a curved blade
4. Craft knife
5. Cocktail sticks
6. Cutting board
7. Tweezers
8. Foam pad
9. Clear silicone sealant
10. Polythene bags
11. Clear varnish
12. PVA glue
13. Mounting board
14. Picture frames
15. Frame mounts
16. Brown paper gummed strip
17. String
18. Sheets of white A4 thick paper or thin card
19. Thin strips of wood
20. Pliers
21. Hacksaw
22. Bradawl
23. Small bowl of water
24. Sticky-backed plate hangers
25. Brooch back
26. Small beads
27. Ribbon
28. Eyelets

The Technique

You do not have to be artistic to enjoy this lovely craft, just a little creative, but before you start buying giftwrap or prints, see if you have kept any old birthday or Christmas cards, as they may have nicely drawn leaves with which you can practise. Ideally, the card should be quite thin, as it will be easier to mould and will therefore provide the best results. Once you have located a card with leaves in the design, try the project below – it will help you to become familiar with the technique.

Instructions

STEP 1

1 Take your card or print and, using a curved-bladed pair of manicure scissors, cut very carefully around the leaf design until you have cut out the entire leaf.

2 Turn the leaf over and place it onto a soft, foam pad (a computer mouse mat is ideal). Holding your scissors carefully by the blade end, use the handle as a shaping tool to rub the back of the leaf using a circular motion. You will notice the leaf curl. Now try painting it with clear varnish. This will give the leaf an enamelled appearance.

3 If you have another leaf, treat it in the same way, but this time put a small amount of silicone sealant on the back and position it so that it overlaps the first leaf.

4 You now have three-dimensional leaves. To finish, apply a coat of varnish to the second leaf.

How much varnish you use depends on how shiny you want your découpage to look. The more glue you use, though, the stronger your work will be. Personally, I like to use plenty of glue to hold my work together, as paper does not tolerate damp conditions and I try to ensure that my designs will not warp, even if they are hung in a steamy kitchen or bathroom. There are one or two exceptions, however, which you will find later in the book.

Some of the most exquisite designs are printed on giftwrap and they, too, make excellent subjects to practise with. The paper does need added strength, but this can be achieved by using PVA to glue the wrapping paper to another sheet of paper or thin card. When the paper dries it will be quite tough, so you must work quickly while the glue is still damp to be able to mould the pieces to the desired shape.

Safety warning: Make sure you always follow the health and safety instructions on any glue and varnish you use, and ensure you have adequate ventilation in your working area.

The
Projects

~

Gerbera

~

The single-flowered gerbera is an ideal subject for découpage, as the petal layers are easy to see and therefore easy to separate. If you use your curved-bladed nail scissors to cut the pieces out, while carefully following the cutting guide, you should find it quite easy to sculpt. As the flower head is large, I do recommend you back each print with another sheet of paper. This will help to keep your gerbera moulded in the desired shape for years to come.

Instructions

THIS PROJECT REQUIRES SIX PRINTS

1 To begin, cut out the entire flower head. The gerbera has four layers of petals. This will be used for the outer layer and will also provide the base for the rest of the flower.

2 Turn the flower over onto a soft, foam pad and rub it with the handle of your scissors. This will make the petals curl slightly, helping to achieve the three-dimensional effect.

5 Look at the cutting guide on page 17 and you will see that the third layer is much easier to cut around (3). Once it is cut out, mould and glue it to the top of the other layers.

6 Next, very carefully cut out the small petals surrounding the yellow pollen in the centre (4), then mould, glue and place them in their correct position.

3 Put a bead of silicone sealant on the back, then place the flower head onto a polythene bag with the design facing upwards.

4 Look at the cutting guide on page 16 and cut the next print in the same way, but this time omit the outer layer of petals (2). This is the most awkward layer because the petals are few, and partly hidden. Mould the petals, then spread silicone sealant on the back of the design. Now place it on top of the first layer.

STEP 4

STEP 6

7 The fifth and sixth prints are used to dress the flower. Cut out the outer rim of the pollen, the folds in the petals and the last tiny pink petal (5), then glue them to the outer layer of the yellow centre. Your flower head is now complete.

8 The leaves and stem are quite simple. Carefully cut out the stem, complete with the leaf attached (6). Rub the stem with the handle of your scissors in a downwards motion, then use a circular motion to rub the leaf.

9 Cut out the largest of the remaining leaves (7) and treat it in the same way. Place the top end of the stem under your completed flower head and position the second leaf at the base of the stem.

10 Take another print and cut out the final leaf, as shown on the guide (8). Mould it and then glue it to the top of the first leaf, so that it overlaps slightly.

11 To achieve the porcelain effect, apply two coats of varnish. Finally, leave it to set on the polythene bag, overnight if possible. It will peel off easily in the morning and will be set hard, ready for you to frame.

STEP 10

STEP 11

© Rob Pohl

Cutting Guide

1

2

3

4

5

6

7

8

Blue Pansies

❧

Pansies are one of the easiest flowers to découpage, and are therefore ideal for beginners. In the following project I have chosen to use 'Blue Pansies' by the artist Bryan Hall.

Instructions

THIS PROJECT REQUIRES FIVE PRINTS

1 Examine your first print and compare it to step one of the cutting guide (*see* page 21). You will notice I have cut away some of the petals. This is to avoid the layered look and will help your work appear more realistic when complete. Using your manicure scissors, cut out your print in the same way.

2 To hide the white cut edges, colour them with a pale green felt-tipped pen.

3 Turn the piece over and place it onto your foam pad. Rub it gently with the handle of your scissors to make the paper curl.

4 Lay this first piece onto a polythene bag and make

a start with the flowers. To avoid confusion, cut out the petals of one flower at a time. Do not throw away the surplus petals; they will be useful as spares if you make an error.

5 Look carefully at your second print. Starting with the pansy on the far left of the design, cut out the first section of the flower, as shown on the guide (2). Now turn it over and mould it with the handle of your scissors.

6 Using a cocktail stick as an applicator, smear the back with silicone sealant and place it gently in its correct position on top of the leaves.

7 Cut out the next piece (3) from another print and treat it in the same way.

8 Using an additional print, cut out the side petals (4) and, once again, treat them in the same manner.

9 Finally, cut the bottom petal (5), sculpt it and lay it in place. You have now completed one pansy.

10 Using the same method, work on one pansy at a time until you have completed all four. Finally, cut out the pieces needed to build up the buds and tiny fold in the leaf on the left.

11 You will be left with several spare leaves. Don't throw them away. Put some extra ones in your picture and save the others for another time; they will come in useful, if only for practise.

12 Usually I recommend you apply plenty glaze to your work. However, for this project I suggest you do not apply any glaze at all, as I have found that it affects the colour of this particular print, making the pansies a much darker blue.

13 To complete your picture, incorporate a blue mount and a frame of your choice. (For details on how to frame see page 95.)

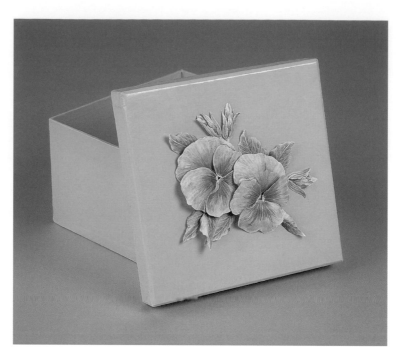

The pansies are ideal for decorating various other items. For instance, the pale blue of the flowers looks extremely effective against the yellow background of this gift box, pictured above.

Cutting Guide

1

2   3

4   5

Pink Pansy Brooch

This attractive brooch can be worn to add impact to a variety of garments. It is very simple to make and is an ideal gift for a special occasion.

For a cutting guide, please refer to steps 2–5 on page 21.

Instructions

THIS PROJECT REQUIRES FIVE PRINTS

1 Using PVA glue, secure the first print to a piece of thin card. Cut out the entire pink pansy. This will form the back of the brooch. Discard the rest of the print.

2 Glue the remaining prints to sheets of thin card or thick paper.

3 Using each of the prints as necessary, cut out the pink pansy's petals in the same way as illustrated on the cutting guide for the blue pansies.

4 Mould the petals very slightly so that they do not protrude too much.

5 Glue the petals to the pansy you cut out in step one, starting with the back petals, then the side petals and finally, the bottom front petal. Leave it to dry for approximately two hours.

6 When the brooch has dried, turn it over and glue a small piece of mounting board (cut carefully with a craft knife) to the back. Leave it to dry, preferably overnight.

7 Attach a brooch pin to the mounting board, using a small quantity of silicone sealant.

8 Apply several coats of glaze to achieve the desired enamelled appearance.

Hydrangeas

This is a beautiful project that can easily be turned into a three-dimensional picture without buying prints.

You will need a box of watercolour paints, a small paintbrush and a couple of large sheets of plain paper. A cutting guide is not required.

Instructions

1 Before you begin, look at the petals of a real hydrangea. You will see that each floret, when pressed flat, is shaped almost like a square, being made up of only four petals. Practise drawing the petals in pairs.

2 For best results, use pink, pale blue and lilac paint, strongly diluted, to cover a large piece of paper with pairs of petals. Use a deeper colour to paint a small dot in between the petals. Cover another piece of paper in the same way.

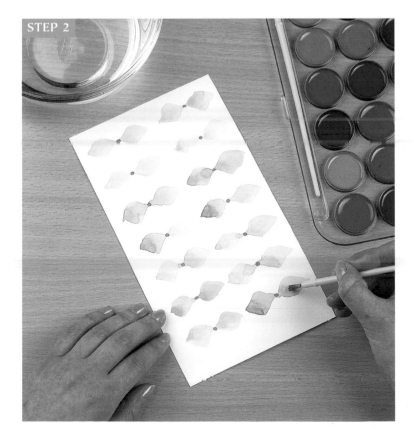

5 While the glue is still damp, cut out the petals and mould them with your fingers. Continue in the same way with the remaining petals, but only do a few at a time in case the glue dries too quickly.

6 When the petals have hardened, glue them together so that each one forms a cross on the mounting board. Make sure you stick enough petals on to overlap the edges.

3 While you are waiting for the paint to dry, cut out a circle of mounting board or thick card that is approximately the size of a large teacup rim. This will make an appropriate base for your petals.

4 Once the petals have dried, roughly cut round four sets. Using a little PVA glue, adhere them to another sheet of paper to increase their strength.

STEP 6

7 Once every area of mounting board has been obscured, apply a second layer of petals.

8 When you are satisfied with your flower head, apply several coats of varnish.

9 Before the varnish dries, an optional touch is to place a tiny pink or blue bead in the centre of each floret. They will adhere to the glaze and look extremely effective.

STEP 4

10 To replicate the picture shown at the start of this project, you will need to create another flower head in just the same way, but using bluer tones of paint.

11 The leaves are a little more difficult. I traced over some leaves that I found in my garden, but you could always cut some out from gardening magazines, stick them to a piece of card with PVA, then mould them while they are still moist.

12 To display the picture, I used an antique pine frame, a green and cream double-sided mount and a dark green background.

As an alternative to framing the hydrangeas, you could use them to decorate a gift box, such as the one above.

Morning-glory Side Table

The top and legs of this side table are made from seasoned elm, and the centre, which measures 26 x 14in (664 x 356mm), is of toughened glass. The morning-glory three-dimensional design in the centre is sculpted from the work of the artist Rob Pohl.

There is no doubt that this project is time consuming to complete, but the end result is worth the effort. If you find the stamens problematic to cut out, they can be replaced with plastic stamens. These can usually be purchased in a variety of colours from shops that sell cake decorations, but if you are only able to find white, they can be coloured with a felt-tipped pen.

Instructions

THIS PROJECT REQUIRES TWELVE PRINTS

1 Using your first print, cut out the back petals and stem of the flower that appears on the right-hand side of the design, as shown on the cutting guide on page 31 (1).

2 Loosen the two back petals by making a downwards cut towards the stamen. Mould the petals and then place them to one side.

3 Use the next print to cut out the side petals (2). Once again, mould them and put them to one side. Discard the stamens – we will use the artificial ones.

4 Taking another print, cut out the front petal (3).

5 You are now ready to assemble the flower.

Spread the back of the side petals with silicone sealant, using enough to elevate the petals slightly, then position them on top of the back petals.

6 Next, glue two artificial stamens on top, making sure that they cover the stamens on the illustration.

7 When you put the front petal in place you will need to elevate it even more, so use a big globule of sealant and leave it to dry on the polythene bag.

8 To make the smaller flower will you need to cut out the entire flower, stem and leaf from the first print and the carpel and petal folds from the second print, then mould and glue them into position (4).

9 Using the extra prints, add as many flowers, leaves and buds to your picture as you wish (5).

Cutting Guide

Butterflies and Wild Flowers

~

This attractive hedgerow is made from giftwrap. An amount of intricate cutting is required, but do not let that deter you – it is not too difficult.

The pattern on the giftwrap is repeated several times, so you should only need one sheet of paper. Do remember, though, to increase its strength by adhering the piece you intend to cut to another sheet of paper using PVA glue.

This hedgerow can also be used as a backdrop for another subject, such as the two teddy bears, shown on page 48.

Instructions

1 Starting with the blue daisy, you will need to cut out two heads and one centre, as shown on the guide on page 35 (1). As daisy petals are quite flat, you will only need to mould them a little. Glue the two daisy heads together and then position the centre of the flower on top.

2 Place the completed daisy on a polythene bag for later attention and make a start on the dog rose.

3 The dog rose will only need one layer of petals and a centre. Cut out the pieces and then mould them with your fingers until you are satisfied with the result (2).

4 Cut out the leaves, as shown on the guide (3), then mould them and put them also to one side on the polythene bag.

5 The blue butterfly has three layers to make its body protrude further than its wings (4). Firstly, cut out the body, feelers and bottom set of

wings. Then, cut out another body and the top wings. Finally, cut out just the body. Now glue them on top of one another in the same order.

6 For the crocus, you need to cut out one complete flower, the stamens and the little fold in the petal (5). Mould the petals towards you with your fingers while the glue is still damp, put the stamens in place and then, lastly, the fold in the petal. For the time being, put it to one side with the daisy, dog rose and butterfly.

7 The final two flowers are, if you look at the cutting guide (6), self-explanatory.

No layers are necessary, just a little cutting and moulding.

8 Repeat these steps to create as many flowers and butterflies as you wish, then arrange them to form an attractive display. Apply glaze for the finishing touch.

Cutting Guide

Honeysuckle Fairy

~

This beautiful honeysuckle fairy would make an ideal picture for a child's bedroom. She looks particularly striking displayed in an antique pine frame and a pale green oval mount.

Instructions

THIS PROJECT REQUIRES FOUR PRINTS

1 If you look at the print you will see that the fairy is standing slightly sideways, with one leg behind the other. So, following the guide on page 39, you will need to cut around her wings, hair, dress and back leg, and cut off her arms and front leg (1).

2 With the second print, cut away her wings, some of her hair and her back leg, and cut around her face, arms and front leg (2). Now, mould the pieces, then place the piece cut from print two on top of the piece cut from print one, and then look at the effect. If you are happy with the result, glue them together with a thin layer of silicone sealant.

3 Use print three to dress her, just like the cardboard dressing-up dolls we used to play with as children (see page 40). Cut out her dress, shoes, wisps of hair and anything else you think might enhance the picture, and then mould and glue them in place (3).

4 Use one more print to cut out her belt, puff-sleeves and the fold in the front of her dress (4).

5 Next, you will need to start cutting out the sprays of honeysuckle decoration (see page 41). This requires intricate cutting and may take a while, but don't be put off, as the result is very rewarding. I recommend you use a backing sheet, as the stems and flowers are particularly delicate and will need extra support. To begin, cut out the stems from the first print, including the leaves and flowers, as shown on the guide (5). Cut out the stamens as well, if you can, but if you find that too difficult, simply cut them off.

6 Rub the back of the stems and flowers with the handle of your scissors to make the honeysuckle lift a little, then place it onto a polythene bag ready to dress.

7 Use the second print to cut out the flowers, omitting the leaves (6), then mould, glue and place on the top of the spray that is waiting on the polythene bag.

8 Now take a third print and cut out the buds from the centre of the flowers, the little curled tips of the flower petals, plus any extra leaves you may wish to use (7).

9 Dress the flower sprays up as much as you can by moulding and gluing even the tiniest of pieces.

10 If, earlier, you found the stamens too difficult to cut out, you could try tiny strands of yellow thread dipped in nail varnish as an alternative.

Cutting Guide

1

2

3

4

7

6

7

7

7

7

5

6

6

7

Sweet Pea Fairy

~

This fairy would also make a lovely picture for a child's bedroom. She is slightly more complicated, as she is wearing a dress that has several folds in the material, but if you follow the cutting guide you shouldn't find her too difficult to make, and I'm sure you'll be pleased with the result.

Instructions

THIS PROJECT REQUIRES FIVE PRINTS

1 Take a good look at the cutting guide for print one (*see* page 45). You will see that I have cut away the fairy's arms and right leg, level with the fold in her dress (1). Do the same, and then mould in the usual way. Put a blob of silicone sealant on the back to hold it in position and place it onto a polythene bag.

2 Using a second print, cut the fairy out again. This time, though, do not remove her arms, but do omit her wings, some of the folds in her skirt and her left foot (2). Mould and spread sealant on the back, then put it in place on top of the piece you cut out from print one.

3 Continue to follow the guide (*see* page 46), using print three for her face, more of her hair, parts of her dress and her left leg (3), and print four for the flowers in her hair, her right leg, the tiny fold on the left side of her skirt, and the bodice of her dress (4). Mould and glue all the pieces except the bodice. We will use it in the next step.

4 From print five add a few extra folds in the skirt of her dress (5), then add the bodice from print four.

5 When you get as far as the sweet pea swing (*see* page 47), I recommend you use a backing sheet before you

cut, as the stems are very fragile. Cut out the swing using the same method as used for the honeysuckle fairy (*see* steps 5–9, pages 37–38), with just one layer for each side of the swing (6).

6 Using some of the scraps, cut out a few extra petals, leaves and buds (7).

7 Finally, mould, glue and place the extra pieces on top of the swing to make it three-dimensional.

8 Apply two or three coats of varnish and leave to dry. Your picture will then be ready to frame.

Cutting Guide

1

2

3

5

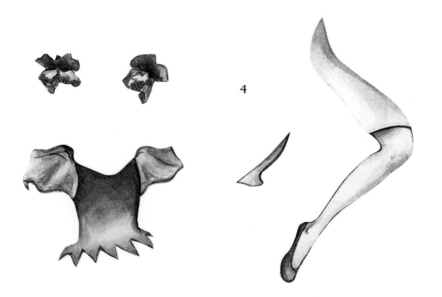

4

Teddy Bears

Teddy bears are popular with young and old alike. To make these characterful bears you will need just two sheets of giftwrap.

As with all giftwrap three-dimensional pictures, you must back the paper with thick paper or thin card, otherwise it will not be strong enough to hold the shape you require and will collapse as soon as the first coat of varnish is applied.

You can use this method of découpage for most prints of bears, but if the bears are clothed you will need at least two extra prints: one for a jacket and another for turned cuffs and collars, etc.

To create the scenery surrounding the bears I incorporated the design from the 'Butterflies and Wild Flowers' project (*see* pages 33–36), plus a few tiny stones and some dried lichen.

Instructions for the dark brown bear

1 Taking the first and second print, cut out the whole bear. Snip around the outlines of both to give the bears a furry appearance.

2 Mould and shape them with the handle of your scissors, then spread the back of one of the pieces with a thin layer of silicone sealant and place it carefully on top of the other piece. This will give the bear some depth.

3 Look at the cutting guide for print three (*see* page 53) and cut out as shown (3), saving the sole of the bear's foot for later use. Once again, snip around the edges and mould and glue in place with the silicone sealant.

4 Take the fourth print and cut out the face, body and right arm, then snip, mould and glue (4). Your bear should now be looking quite chubby.

5 Use the fifth print to cut out the forehead, nose, the pad on the paw and the same sole as the third print (5).

6 It may seem a waste of a print, but you will need to use the sixth print to cut out just the bear's nose, plus some of the surrounding fur (6).

7 Stick one sole to each foot, then snip and glue the pad and facial features in place. Use enough silicone to elevate the nose from the rest of the facial features.

8 For the final touch, add two small black or brown beads for eyes and a small piece of black card for the bear's nose.

9 Apply several coats of glaze and then leave to dry overnight on a polythene bag.

Now try making the honey-coloured bear using the same method and following the second cutting guide.

Cutting Guide

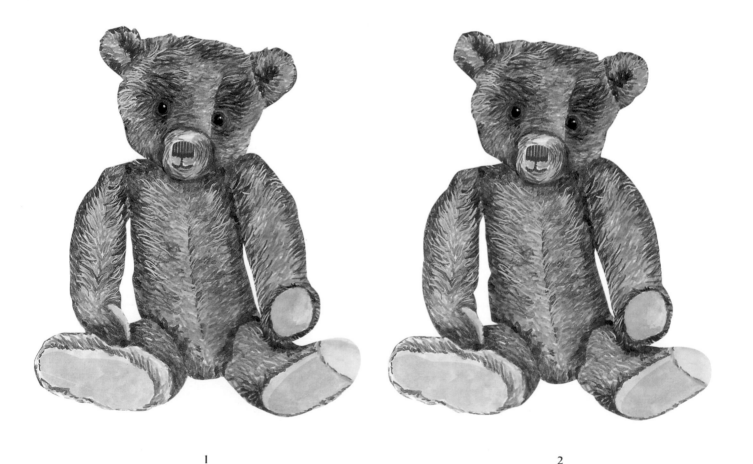

1

2

3

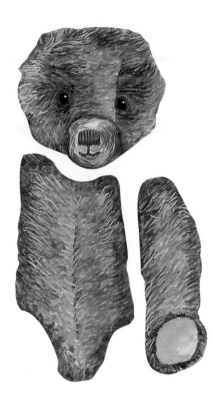

4

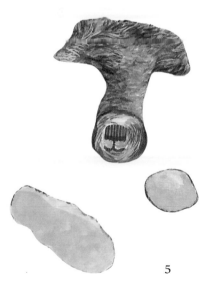

5

6

1

2

3

4

5

6

Hedgehog

This hedgehog is made in a similar way to the bears,
but requires only one sheet of giftwrap.

Instructions

1 Carefully cut around the hedgehog, jug and any part of the surrounding design you wish to include in your picture. Snip around the hedgehog to make the bristles appear spiky.

2 Cut out three faces, reducing them in size, as shown on the cutting guide on page 58 (2), then mould and glue with the silicone sealant, building the face up gradually.

3 Cut out the jug and flowers, then sculpt and layer the pieces (3).

4 Cut out the hedgehog's arm and snip around the edge to provide the spiky effect, then mould, glue, and put in place (4).

5 Now start to work on the sunflowers, building them up in the same order as shown on the guide on page 59 (5). Place the completed flowers slightly over to the left of the picture, covering the bottom of the hedgehog.

6 Cut out several of the tiny pink flowers (6), mould them and then pierce each centre with your scissors to make the flowers appear more lifelike. Position them wherever you think best.

7 Finally, apply several coats of varnish.

Cutting Guide

1

2

3

4

5

6

Pink Fuchsia

The pink fuchsia is a popular design for three-dimensional découpage, and many of you who are familiar with the craft will know it well. However, I am frequently asked for a cutting guide, so here it is. I do recommend you use a backing sheet, as the stems and stamens are delicate and will need support.

This design is also suitable for decorating the side table in the morning-glory project on page 29.

Instructions

THIS PROJECT REQUIRES FIVE PRINTS

1 Look at step one of the guide on page 63. Using all five of your prints, cut out the same pieces.

2 Mould them with your scissors, then, leaving the folds in the petals, the dewdrops and stamens for later use, glue them together with your sealant, following the print as a guide. When you are satisfied with the result, place them on a polythene bag and wait for the sealant to set.

3 While you are waiting, cut out from two prints the bud that is on the far right of the design (2). Mould the back of one of the pieces and make a few snips upwards on the second. Then, rub the back of the second bud and glue it to the first one.

4 Now return to the flower and leaves. Dress them with the dewdrops and folds that you had put to one side.

5 Finally, using a large amount of sealant, put the stamens in place underneath the completed flower and leave to dry before glazing. Remember, you can use more prints to add as many extra flowers, leaves and buds to your picture as you wish.

Cutting Guide

Dahlia

~

This stunning dahlia is another perfect subject for the beginner. For best results I suggest you use a backing sheet to increase the strength of the flower head. To display the dahlia, I recommend you use a simple, cream background.

Instructions

THIS PROJECT REQUIRES SIX PRINTS

1 Look at the cutting guide on page 67. Using your first print, cut out the entire flower head (1).

2 With your second print, cut out the flower head again, but this time omit the outer layer of petals (2). Mould this piece, then glue it on top of the first piece.

3 Following the cutting guide on page 68, cut away the two outer layers of petals on your next print (3). Glue this to the second piece to build up the design.

4 Cut out the centre of the dahlia from your fourth print, including the small surrounding petals (4), then mould, glue and place it in its correct position.

5 Take your fifth print and cut out the small petals that overlap the centre of the flower head (5), then use the rest of the print to embellish your dahlia head with the extra folds in the petals.

6 Next, cut out the stem, with the leaves attached, as shown on the guide on page 69 (6).

7 Take a further print and cut out the larger leaf at the base of the stem (7).

8 Mould the stem by running the handle of your scissors down the length

of the stem, and rub the leaves in a circular motion. Treat the larger leaf in the same way, then glue the leaf in position on top of the stem.

9 To give the larger leaf a greater three-dimensional effect, take another print and cut out the fold (8). Mould this piece, then add a small amount of sealant before placing it on top of the leaf.

10 Using another blob of sealant to secure it, push the top end of the stem into place just underneath the flower.

11 For that final touch, apply two or three coats of varnish.

© Rob Pohl

Cutting Guide

1

2

3

4

5

6

7

8

Greetings Cards

Blank cards are available from many craft shops and are ideal for découpage. It is also possible to buy sheets of adhesive foil labels with greetings on them, including 'Happy Birthday', 'Merry Christmas', 'Thank You' and 'Best Wishes' to add to the cards.

If you are using a print to découpage your card, make sure you choose a design that is small enough to fit within the aperture. Perhaps, if you are artistic, you may wish to design something for the card yourself. Forget-me-nots, for instance, are quite 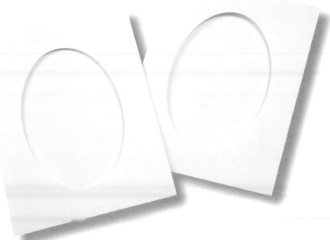 simple to draw, just follow the instructions provided over the page. The red poppy card can be made from Simon Elvin giftwrap.

Do remember that it is best not to elevate the work too much unless you are prepared to make a box, as greetings cards are usually sent in the post and can easily get damaged.

Instructions for the Forget-me-not card

1 Take a small piece of paper and draw a stem, some leaves and several flowers. When you have done this, draw some extra flowers – I suggest about 12. If you are pleased with your artwork and do not wish to spoil it by cutting it up, take it to a printer and ask for it to be colour photocopied on good quality paper.

2 Cut out the whole sprig, and rub the back with the handle of your scissors on a foam pad, then put it to one side. Now cut out the individual extra flowers.

3 Rub the back of the flowers in the usual way, then turn them over and pierce their centres with the point of your scissors.

STEP 1

STEP 4

4 With tweezers, pick up each flower and apply to the back of them a tiny amount of PVA or silicone sealant, using a cocktail stick as an applicator. Position them on top of the sprig of flowers and leave them to dry.

5 Once dry, your forget-me-nots will be ready to glue to a blank card.

Instructions for the Poppy card

1 Before you start, make sure you glue the giftwrap to a backing sheet to give your design increased strength. Now cut out the petal to the left of the flower, including the part that is covered by overlapping petals, as shown on the guide (1). Mould it with your fingers, then place it to one side.

2 Look at the guide and cut out the next piece from your giftwrap in the same way. This time you will need the petal (2) on the right side of the poppy and the petal at the bottom (3). The rest of the cut piece is to be used as a base onto which the other parts can be layered.

3 Put a small amount of silicone sealant onto the back of your second piece and gently glue it on top of the first piece, making sure the petals overlap correctly.

4 Now it is time to work on the centre of the flower. Using a cocktail stick as a tool, place a small amount of

silicone sealant in the middle of your poppy, just enough to cover the seedpod and stamens. Scatter a teaspoon of dried poppy seeds on top of the sealant, then pat them down gently with your finger and leave it to dry for a while.

5 Once dry you can shake off the surplus poppy seeds and start to work on the final front petal. Look again at the guide and you will see it is the one shaped like a crescent. Cut out the petal, mould it carefully and smear plenty of sealant on the back, then glue it in place.

6 Apply two or three coats of varnish and leave it to dry overnight. In the morning your poppy will be ready to glue to a blank greetings card.

Cutting Guide

1

2

3

Orange Poppy

This poppy design is fabulous, and very easy to make into a three-dimensional picture. Although it is printed on high quality paper, I do recommend you back each sheet with thin card or thick paper, as the subject is so large. Try to work quite quickly – if the paper is still damp from the glue, it will be easier to mould into shape.

Instructions

THIS PROJECT REQUIRES FIVE PRINTS

1 You will see from the guide on page 79 that I have cut out the whole flower from the first print, but where the inside petals overlap I have cut inwards slightly. This is to hide the layers when the inside petals are glued into place. Cut out the flower from your first print in the same way (1).

2 Cut out the leaves (2) and put them to one side. Discard the stem.

3 Have a look at the guide on page 80 and cut out the inner petals from your second print in the same way (3). You can also use this print to cut out the folds in the petals from the outer layer, the large leaf, and the stem with the leaf attached (4), leaving a small section of petal at the top.

4 Now sculpt all the pieces. If you used a backing sheet you should be able to mould them with your fingers, but if you didn't you will need to use the handle of your scissors. Cover the back of the inner petals with silicone sealant and place them over the outer petals, then glue and position the petal folds.

5 Use the third print to cut out the petal folds from the inner layer and the petal that is partly hidden in the centre, shown on page 81 (5). Sculpt them and then stick them in place.

6 Before you cut out and stick that last folded petal (6) you must decide what to do with the centre. I decided

STEP 6

off the surplus. If you wish, place a poppy seed head in the centre, too, and gently push it down into the sealant.

7 Now cut out and glue into position the last petal from print four, and the remaining fold shown on the guide from print five (6).

8 Finally, push the stem underneath the outer petals, add as many leaves as you like, then apply several coats of glaze and leave it to dry overnight.

9 If you wish to frame your poppy a dark green mount and an antique pine frame suits it very well.

for this project to incorporate real poppy seeds and the top part of a dried seed pod, but it would look equally good if you used tiny black or yellow beads. Smear enough sealant to cover the centre, then sprinkle a teaspoon of seeds or beads on top. Pat them down with your fingers, and shake

STEP 7

© Rob' Pohl

Cutting Guide

1

2

3

4

5

6

Nasturtium Wall Plaque

~

Instead of framing these beautiful nasturtiums, I decided to use them to decorate a circular, wooden chopping board to create this striking wall plaque.

Instructions

THIS PROJECT REQUIRES FIVE PRINTS

1 Cut out as many complete leaves as you can from all five prints (*see* step one of the cutting guide on page 85), then mould them slightly with the handle of your scissors.

2 Where some of the leaves are partly obscured by petals, cut them out as shown on the guide (2). Later, they can be covered with the completed flowers, leaving just the leaves on display.

3 The flowers may look difficult, but I can assure you they are actually quite simple. Cut out the petals, following the guide (3), mould them and then layer the petals in the same order as they appear in the print.

4 Now look at the print on page 84 and assemble your leaves and flowers in a similar way, using PVA glue to adhere the pieces to your chopping board.

5 Apply a coat of varnish and leave to dry.

6 For a final touch, you could hang your wall plaque with a brightly coloured ribbon, as I have done here.

Cutting Guide

Mushroom Wall Tile

~

This mushroom wall tile makes an attractive kitchen adornment.
I chose to use a plain white tile, but the design would look equally
effective on a beige or dark green background.

Instructions

THIS PROJECT REQUIRES FOUR PRINTS

1 Begin by cutting around the edge of the design. I chose to cut off the top of the grass that appears behind the central mushroom, but you can include it if you wish. Mould the design very slightly and then, using PVA glue, stick it directly onto the tile.

2 Using your second print, follow the cutting guide on page 89 and cut out the two mushrooms that are lying either side of the central mushroom (2). Mould them and then glue them to the first print in the same position. Save the remaining pieces from the print for later use.

3 The third print is used for the central mushroom only, which brings it forward from the rest of the design (3). Again, save the rest of the print for later decoration.

4 The fourth print provides the embellishment for the mushrooms (4). Place another layer on the red caps of the mushroom heads and the frill on the central stem.

5 Once the mushrooms are completed, use the spare pieces left over from the prints to decorate the background, alongside the leaves and acorns (5). Use as many extra pieces

as you like and remember, they don't have to go back in their original positions. You can also use any surplus pieces to cover up areas if you have snipped a little bit too enthusiastically.

6 A sticky-backed plate hanger, obtainable from hardware stores, is ideal for hanging your tile.

Cutting Guide

Decorated Clip-frames

Many people like to frame their photographs, but buying an attractive frame each time can become expensive, so it is usual for some to be framed, others to be sent to friends or relatives, and the rest to be placed in a box and stored at the back of a cupboard.

Clip-frames are an effective alternative to the usual photograph frames. They are inexpensive and can easily be enhanced with a little découpage stuck directly onto the glass. Cleaning is simple – all you need is a soft brush to keep the dust at bay.

Frame 1

This clip-frame, with a photograph of the rascals in my family, is decorated with spring flowers taken from a sheet of giftwrap. I have prepared a cutting guide for you to follow. As usual, I strengthened the subject by backing it onto another sheet of paper, and cut out and moulded the petals while they were still damp. Finally, I applied several layers of varnish.

Frame 2

Being a bridesmaid was a very serious occasion for the three-year-old in this picture. And, of course, she stole the show in her frock that was too big for her and her head-dress that kept slipping down over her eyes. The decoration I chose to enhance the clip-frame was made from scraps of flowers left over from the Sweet Pea Fairy project (*see* pages 43–47). The delicate flowers were perfect for this treasured photograph.

Frame 3

The honeysuckle decoration on the frame of this old black and white photograph is made from left over pieces from the Honeysuckle Fairy project (*see* pages 37–41). I used translucent yellow nail varnish to enhance the colour.

Cutting Guide

Framing

To frame the projects in this book you will require frames with deep recesses. Such frames are available but tend to be expensive. A cheaper and simple alternative is to adapt standard frames.

Instructions

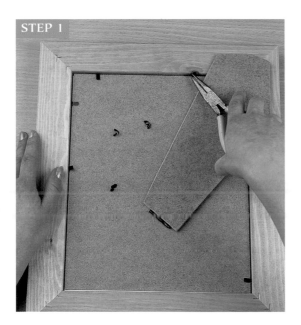

3 On the back of the frame, apply a small quantity of PVA glue to the corner of each recess.

1 Remove the cellophane wrapping from the frame and, using pliers, take out the pins from the back.

2 Take out the glass and put it to one side, ready for cleaning.

4 Return to the glass and clean it thoroughly on both sides with a glass cleaner, then carefully place it back into the recess of the frame, making sure you do not leave any finger marks.

5 Place a suitable mount face down on the glass and get ready to make a box for the back. Stripwood is ideal for this and is obtainable from most DIY stores.

6 Hold a strip of wood against the recess in the frame and mark the length to be cut with a pencil. Using a small saw (a hacksaw is ideal), cut off the measured length.

7 Check the piece you have cut is the correct size by trying it out in the recess. If

STEP 6

you are sure your measurement is correct, cut another identical piece of wood for the opposite side.

8 Smear PVA glue onto one side of each wooden strip and fit them to the sides of the recess on top of the mount. Measure two more pieces of wood in the same way to go across the width of the frame. Cut again, check again, and glue again.

STEP 7

STEP 8

9 Now take the backing (usually hardboard) from the frame. Place it over a sheet of mounting board as a template and, using a strong craft knife, cut carefully around it.

10 Glue the mounting board directly onto the backing with PVA and then wait for the glue to dry. You have now created a box frame, ready for your three-dimensional picture. The mounting board will make an excellent base for your completed picture. If you use large blobs of silicone sealant to adhere your work it will stop it from being flat against the background.

11 When your picture is dry and ready to be placed in the frame, apply a small amount of PVA to the edge of the wooden strips and run your finger along them to ensure the application is smooth.

12 Check the picture frame once more, paying extra attention to the glass and mount to ensure that no specks of dust or fluff have crept in. Now place your picture on the wooden strips at the back. Leave it face down for a while to dry, and put a heavy book on top to ensure it adheres all the way round.

STEP 11

13 The back of the picture is just as important as the front if you want it to look professional. Do not be tempted to use masking tape to cover the edges, even if it looks acceptable; it is unlikely to last, and you may find that after just a few weeks of

hanging your picture that it falls down and destroys your work. Instead, the best tape to use for sealing the back of a picture is brown paper gummed strip, available from most stationers. Hold the gummed strip against the

length of the box and then cut off an extra inch (2.5cm).

14 Submerge the tape briefly in a bowl of water and shake off the surplus drops – this will make the tape adhesive.

STEP 13

STEP 14

15 Apply the tape to the back of the box so that half of it overlaps the side, and then cut the extra inch (2.5cm) down the centre to the box.

16 Press the strip over the side of the box and bring the extra inch round the corner. Quickly wipe off any excess moisture with a piece of kitchen roll and trim the edges with a craft knife. Continue in in this fashion all the way round the frame.

STEP 17

STEP 15

STEP 18

17 Using a small bradawl, make a hole on either side of the back of the frame and insert a small eyelet into each hole.

18 Screw the eyelets in place until they feel secure and then tie a piece of string to them. Your frame is now complete and your picture can be hung.

Troubleshooting and Useful Tips

When the glue and glaze has dried on your découpage, you may find that some of the surplus glaze has run down onto the polythene bag. If it has spoilt the appearance of your work, you can trim it off with nail scissors, provided the glaze is thoroughly dry.

Wood glue is a suitable alternative if you have difficulty in obtaining PVA glue.

If mounting board is unavailable in your area it can be substituted with thick card.

Many years ago I made a picture using foxglove prints. It still hangs in my living room, and is often admired by my visitors. The colours have not faded or yellowed with age. I used a clear nail varnish for the glaze. So, if you cannot find a varnish specifically designed for craftwork, nail varnish is an effective alternative.

If you drop silicone sealant on your work, leave it to dry for a while. You may be able to peel it away. If this proves impossible, an extra petal or a leaf in a strategic position can help to disguise it.

Try experimenting with colour. I have often used felt-tipped pens to enhance my work. Coloured nail varnish can also be extremely useful to cover up mistakes. (I recommend you experiment with old greetings cards first.)

Suppliers

The pansies, nasturtiums and mushrooms are the work of Bryan Hall who, with his wife Chrissie, produces a lovely collection of prints. The contact address is:

BCH Bryan and Chrissie Hall Greetings Cards
2 Hermitage Close
Westbury
Shropshire
SY5 9QL
U.K.
Telephone: +44 (0)1743 884113

The teddy bears (serial number SE GW 2588), hedgehog, spring flowers (serial number ESE GW 3327), red poppy (serial number SE GW 2557) and wild flowers (serial number SE GW 00546) are from giftwrap designs published by Simon Elvin Ltd, which can be bought from shops and stationers.

The orange poppy, gerbera, dahlia, morning-glory and pink fuchsia are the work of Rob Pohl. The honeysuckle and sweet pea fairies are the work of Sharon Healey. All are published by John Arnold Publishing. The prints can be purchased from:

Jacksons Mail Order
Unit 2
Clarendon Court
Winwick Quay
Warrington
WA2 8QP
U.K.
Telephone: +44 (0)1925 417017

Rob Jackson also supplies kits, picture frames, glue, varnish and tools. His catalogue is a mine of information for three-dimensional découpage.

About the Author

Hilda Stokes has been fascinated by three-dimensional découpage for many years and has spent much of her time perfecting the craft. In addition to the commissions she receives, Hilda provides weekly découpage lessons and gives frequent talks and demonstrations.

Index

TITLES AVAILABLE FROM
GMC Publications
BOOKS

WOODCARVING

WOODTURNING

WOODWORKING

UPHOLSTERY

The above represents a full list of all titles currently published or scheduled to be published.
All are available direct from the Publishers or through bookshops, newsagents and specialist retailers.
To place an order, or to obtain a complete catalogue, contact:

GMC PUBLICATIONS
166 High Street, Lewes, East Sussex BN7 1XU, United Kingdom
Tel: 01273 488005 Fax: 01273 478606
E-mail: pubs@thegmcgroup.com

Orders by credit card are accepted